KILLING WARSAW

The Full True Story of The City That Was to Disappear

KRIS TRELSKI

To my wife Halina and my sons Michal, Tomasz, Grzegorz
and Jacek who inspired me to write this book.

"The city must completely disappear from the surface of the earth" -
Heinrich Himmler

Killing Warsaw

CONTENTS

INTRODUCTION

On the 1st of September 1939 Warsaw had 1,300,000 inhabitants. After 5 years of brutal German occupation on August 1, 1944 there were 900,000 people. On the 1st of January 1945 Warsaw had no more than 1,000 inhabitants.

Theater Square (Public Domain)

In January 1945, Warsaw was a sea of ruins. What had once been one of the most beautiful cities in Central Europe was now a wasteland. Its cultural treasures had either been stolen or deliberately destroyed; its architectural gems reduced to blackened rubble.

"About 90% of Warsaw's buildings had been demolished and most of its population murdered, significantly greater destruction than was caused by the atomic bombs in Hiroshima and Nagasaki." - Steve Hochstadt, History News Network.

The devastation of the city was almost total, and the new Communist authorities even considered naming another city Poland's capital instead. According to one idea, Warsaw was to be left the way it was as a war memorial and a warning for future generations.

The Royal Castle in 1945 (Public Domain)

No modern city had ever been rebuilt after such complete demolition, but Polish patriots argued that the historical substance of Warsaw represented the Polish nation and should be rebuilt. The destruction of the city center was so complete that 22 paintings of city streets done in the 1770s by the Venetian painter Bernardo Bellotto were used to recreate historic buildings. Bricks from the rubble and fragments of architectural details were reused. It took over 7 years to rebuild the city.

PRE-WAR PLAN

The destruction of the city of Warsaw was planned long before its almost total destruction in 1944, even prior to the start of World War II.

On 20 June 1939, Adolf Hitler was presented with a plan called "German town – Warschau". The plan included architectural plans and models of a city that resembled a typical mid-size German town. The plans were prepared by an architectural bureau in Würzburg and later became known as the Pabst Plan.

Friedrich Pabst prepared a technical plan for the annihilation of Warsaw and the complete ethnic cleansing of its native Polish population, with Polish Jews condemned to be the first destined for extermination. It envisaged the transformation of the Polish capital into a new, provincial German town, containing an exclusively ethnic German population of no more than 130,000 people on the left bank supported by a slave labor camp of 80,000 Poles on the right bank of the Vistula. Since Warsaw's total population in 1935 was around 1.3 million that meant that 94% of them were to be removed or exterminated. The plans included drawings and photos, and other documentation. Among the documents was a colored plan of the future town which was created by German architects in 1:20, 000 scale titled The New German City, Warschau.

Some documents of the project were based on Polish documentation from 1935 developed by professor O. Sosnowski obtained by German "scientists" under the false pretense of scientific research into city's historical development. German scholars, historians, conservators and professors of architecture, and other experts were enlisted to catalogue all the most important and culturally significant landmarks of the city, the most exquisite churches and public buildings, key library collections, artworks, and sculptures.

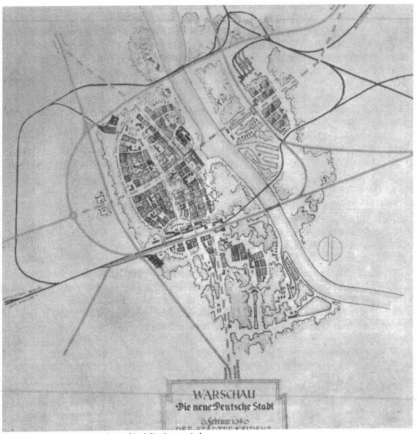

German town – Warschau (Public Domain)

The "German Warschau" was planned to be built on the crossroad of German highways and railroad networks. It covered 2.3 square miles (6 km²) built-up area plus 0.4 square miles (1 km²) of Warsaw's centuries-old Prague district, for a combined 2.7 square mile area plus some parks and green areas. It represented 1/20 of the existing Polish capital city and was very different from the actual existing road network of 1939. The whole town center was to be built into a net of narrow, picturesque streets, resembling the planning of a typical German town. The modern and wide Polish capital avenues would have been erased forever with all their monuments and beautiful buildings and palaces. Only the remains of the

4

Old Town district (without the Polish King's Castle), the King's Baths Palace, the Belvedere - the residence of the heads of state, and modified parts of the Vistula riverside buildings would have been saved.

The evidence of pre-planned destruction, or should we say the premeditated killing, of the city was nonexistent or lost, or simply well-hidden until recently when Polish researcher bought on Ebay two sets of German documents from 1939. They documented, with typical accuracy, the step-by-step progress of the destruction of the city, including the civilian targets like bridges, railroad stations, hospitals, libraries, and the Jewish sections of the city. As "The Telegraph" reported on the find: *"the first (set) contains plans and maps from before the war detailing potential targets even in some cases stating the thickness of the walls. The second one has 100 pictures of destroyed buildings in what appears to be an assessment by the Germans of their plans."*

What the researchers found interesting is the fact that those documents do not include any assessments of military installations like garrisons or ammunition depots. That suggests that the all the damages to the civilian targets during military operations were not incidental.

On the 1st of September 1939 Warsaw had 1,300,000 inhabitants.

SEPTEMBER '39

From September 1 to September 6, Warsaw was defended by Air Force unit, the Pursuit Brigade, as well as by the units of the Warsaw Antiaircraft Defense mostly manned by city residents. On September 3, Minister of Military Affairs, General Kasprzycki, ordered General Czuma to organize the defense of the city against the armored assault.

Warsaw 1939 (Fotopolska.eu / Deutsches Bundesarchiv)

The anti-aircraft defenses started to crumble when on September 5 by order of the military authorities 11 AA batteries were withdrawn from Warsaw towards the eastern cities of Lublin, Brześć and Lwów. Soon after the German high command, seeing less danger to their own aircraft, redirected more bombers to attack the city, especially the historical old town, the Warsaw Royal Castle and other iconic monuments, significant to the Polish nation and its capital. Almost at the same time the crews of the German planes started to attack civilians using machine guns while flying at lower altitudes.

Starting from September 6, the formation of civil defense and the Workers' Defense Brigade of Warsaw began. On September 6, shortly before midnight, the head of propaganda in the Staff of the Supreme Commander, Colonel Umiastowski called on the radio for residents of Warsaw to participate in the construction of barricades and fortifications in the face of the direct threat to the city by the Germans. At the same time, he urged all men capable of carrying weapons, not called up to the army, to leave the capital without delay and go east, where they were to be mobilized. Even before dawn on September 7, thousands of people started to leave Warsaw eastwards. On the same day, September 7th, all the government officials as well as military high command left the city to avoid encirclement and continue the fight. The commissioner president of the city Stefan Starzyński became the highest civilian authority.

The Germans tried to capture the capital by surprise with the forces of two panzer divisions (1st and 4th Panzer Divisions), which on September 6th successfully broke the Polish front near Piotrków and Tomaszów. On September 8th the elements of the German 4th Panzer Division took Okęcie airport, and by the evening they reached the outskirts of Warsaw where they came into contact with the defenders. However, the Germans withdrew postponing the attack for the next day.

On September 10, there were more than 70 German bombers above Warsaw. During that day, nicknamed "Bloody Sunday", there were 17 consecutive bombing raids. Around the same Polish authorities begun to note that the display of "Red Cross" flags marking the hospitals, contrary to their purpose, became the targets of the bombings. It also became clear that planes begun to avoid defended military targets attacking instead schools, theaters, hospitals, residential buildings, and even churches. In other words, any location that may have a high concentration of civilians became the target for German pilots.

On September 13-15, the city was completely encircled. By the order of the Polish Supreme Commander, the "Warsaw" Army was established under the command of General Rómmel. Stefan Starzyński appointed the Citizens' Committee at the Command of the Defense of Warsaw, bringing together representatives of all political groups in the Republic. On September 17-22, the Warsaw garrison was strengthened by units of the "Poznań" Army and the "Pomerania" Army, which after the Battle of Bzura through the Kampinos Forest broke into the capital.

The Royal Castle - September 17 (Public Domain)

On September 17, after the USSR's aggression against Poland, Adolf Hitler, who was near Warsaw, issued a personal order to fire at the Royal Castle to force the Polish capital to surrender. The capitulation of Warsaw was an agreed German-Soviet condition for the partition of the territory of the Polish state between the Third Reich and the Soviet Union. As a consequence, the German army escalated attacks (contrary to the Hague Convention) directed against the civilian population of Warsaw and intended to force the city to surrender as soon as possible.

On September 25, also known as the Black Monday, starting at 8:00am a carpet bombing was carried out by the Luftwaffe on Warsaw. About 10,000 civilians were killed that day, 35,000 were injured, and 12% of the city's buildings were destroyed. At the time the raid was considered the largest and deadliest air raid in history. It lasted 11 hours during which German planes performed 1,150 sorties, dropping 560 tons of high explosive bombs and 72 tons of incendiary bombs. The Luftwaffe bombed the Warsaw gas plant, power plant and water filtering station. In the absence of power, the Warsaw II radio station broadcasting from Fort Mokotowski fell silent. These attacks were an introduction to the general assault on the city, on September 26 German troops carried out an attack, which, however, did not bring them much success. In the last days of the siege the defense forces still had around 3,000 officers and over 82,000 soldiers. However, they have begun to run out of ammunition. On September 26, a decision was made to surrender to Germany due to the situation of the civilian population. The capitulation act of the capital was signed on September 28 at the site of the former Skoda Air Engine Factory in Okęcie Airport.

urvivor of bombing of Warsaw, photographed by Julien Bryan (Public Domain)

On September 27, German troops entered the city. It is estimated that during the Warsaw Siege between 20,000 and 25,000 civilians were killed, 40 percent of the buildings in the city were damaged and 10 percent of the buildings destroyed. Some of the damage was the result of ground artillery fire, including intense street fighting between German infantry and armor units and Polish infantry and artillery, and not solely caused by aerial bombing.

According to the Germans and their implementation of the laws of war, Warsaw was a defended military target and the Luftwaffe raids could be construed as a legitimate military operation.

On September 28, 1939 - immediately after the capitulation of Warsaw the pact of friendship was between the Third Reich and the Soviet Union was finalized in Moscow establishing, contrary to international law (Hague Convention IV of 1907), German-Russian border on the occupied territory of Poland. On October 5, 1939, Adolf Hitler received a parade of German troops on the streets of Warsaw.

OCCUPATION

On October 1, 1939, a five-year occupation of Warsaw has begun. The city lost its status as a capital and became part of the General Governorate. From the first days of occupation, the Germans used brutal terror against the capital's population, aimed primarily at representatives of the Polish political and intellectual elites, the Jewish community and people in any way associated with the resistance movement.

Wawer Massacre (Public Domain)

The first massacre of occupied Warsaw took place on the night of December 26, 1939. On the evening of that day, two known Polish criminals, Marian Prasuła and Stanisław Dąbek, killed two German non-commissioned officers from Baubataillon 538. After learning of it, the

11

acting commander of the Ordnungspolizei in Warsaw, colonel Max Daume ordered an immediate reprisal, consisting of a series of arrests of random Polish males, aged 16 to 70, found in the region where the killings occurred (in Wawer and the neighboring Anin villages). 107 Polish civilians were killed that night (114 shot, of whom 7 survived).

The principle of collective responsibility was commonly used under various pretexts. As a result, Warsaw's prisons and detention centers such as Pawiak Prison and Gestapo Headquarters at Szucha Avenue were soon overfilled with prisoners.

Pawiak Prison (Pawiak) built in 1829–35 was the main prison of central Poland before the war. In 1939, it became Gestapo's prison. Approximately 100,000 people were imprisoned there, some 37,00 died on the premises (executed, under torture, or during detention), and 60,000 were transferred to Nazi concentration camps. The large number of Jews passed through Pawiak but the exact numbers are unknown, as the prison archives were never found.

Gestapo HQ (Public Domain)

The Gestapo Headquarters at Szucha was quite literally the worst place on Earth, ever. After Warsaw's capitulation the Nazis took over the building that before the war housed the Ministry of Religious Beliefs and Public Education and turned it into the Gestapo HQ. In the basement of the building, they set up jails for their victims. Prisoners who were located there were usually freshly caught or transferred from Pawiak prison. They were subject to brutal interrogations, during which they were tortured and severely beaten. When it came to torture there were no exceptions, even pregnant women were beaten and tortured. Polish prisoners often scratched out some sentences about beatings into the prison walls. Many of these inscriptions were personal, patriotic or religious. In the 1960s research was conducted, and over 1,000 texts were conserved. The most famous of them is the following:

It is easy to speak about Poland.
It is harder to work for her.
Even harder to die for her.
And the hardest to suffer for her.

Many of the prisoners were killed during interrogations or died as a result of their injuries. During the Warsaw Uprising, the Germans mass executed thousands of Poles in the surrounding areas. Their corpses were later burned in neighboring buildings. The extent of these killings were tremendous, human ashes found in the basement after the war weighed 5,578.5 kg (12,298 lb.).

Pawiak inmates hanged by the Gestapo on February 11, 1944

After the war the people of Warsaw treated the place as a cemetery, often bringing flowers and lighting candles. In July 1946 the Polish government decided to designate the site as a place of martyrdom. It was decided that the jails would remain untouched and turned into a museum. It was opened on 18 April 1952. Hallways, four group cells and ten solitary cells were preserved in their original condition. In accordance with the testimonies of prisoners, a room of a Gestapo officer was recreated. Several tons of human ashes found there were relocated to the Warsaw Insurgents Cemetery. Museum visitors must be at least 14 years old.

For a long time, Germans carried out executions of prisoners from Warsaw in secret, in the area inaccessible to bystanders. Places of execution were, among others: Seym (Parliament) Gardens; Kabaty Woods; so called "Swedish Mountains" in Bemowo; Sękociński Forest near Magdalenka; Chojnow Woods near Stefanów; the outskirts of Kampinos Forest; and above all - the Palmiry village - the site of a series of mass executions.

After the suppression of the Ghetto uprising on May16, 1943 the areas of the former "Jewish residential district" were transformed by the German forces into a "stone-brick desert". The leaders of Gestapo came to a conclusion that the ruins of the ghetto might turn out to be a convenient place to carry out secret executions of Poles – this time on a massive scale. From their point of view, a number of factors spoke in favor of using the ruins of the ghetto as a place of mass executions. The district was directly adjacent to the Pawiak prison where the vast majority of Polish political prisoners were detained. The ghetto walls and numerous German posts completely isolated the "stone and brick desert" from the rest of the city. Police patrols constantly hunted Jews hiding in the ruins, which explained the sound of shots coming from behind the walls. It was easy to bury or burn the bodies of the murdered in the ruins.

The information on German crimes provided to the outside by the members of the underground employed at Pawiak as the custodian staff was inevitably fragmented, so it is impossible to determine the exact dates and course of all the murders carried out in the ghetto ruins in the spring and summer of 1943. However, it is known that the executions were carried out almost every day. In most cases it was several to a dozen victims, but there have been cases in which dozens or even hundreds of Poles and Jews have been murdered in individual executions. On May 29, 1943, about 530 people were killed there. The news of the execution spread widely in occupied Warsaw – it was then that the inscriptions "Pawiak pomścimy" (We'll avenge Pawiak) began to appear on a large scale on the walls of the city. On June 24, 1943, about 200 people died in the next big execution in the ghetto. On July 15, 1943, from 260 to 300 people were shot there – Poles and Jews arrested as a result of the so-called "Polish Hotel affair". The next day, 132 more prisoners of Pawiak were executed.

We'll avenge Pawiak (Public Domain)

In addition, between October 1943 and February 1944, the occupiers carried out nearly 35 street executions in Warsaw. The total number of executed victims is estimated at 32,000. In principle, it does not include Jews - victims of the Holocaust (except for those who went through Pawiak and other Warsaw prisons), as well as people tortured in the Gestapo investigation and killed in street shootings or during attempted arrest. In addition, around 60,000 inhabitants of the city were sent to concentration camps during this period, most of them Warsaw intelligentsia - in 1939, there were 122.8 thousand people that could be described as members of the Warsaw intelligentsia (including white-collar workers), in October 1941, only two years later, there were nearly half (61.2 thousand people) that remained.

Mass killings were not the only method of terror in Warsaw. Thousands of Warsaw residents were also sent to the concentration or forced labor (slave) camps. The Germans established a number of camp facilities in Warsaw, collected in 1943 under the name KL Warschau concentration camp, in which, as a sub-camp of Majdanek or for a short time, an independent camp, besides the use of slave labor, there was genocide. While it is estimated that 4,000 to 5,000 Warsovians have died in the camp there is also a theory that asserts that a giant gas chamber was built in a tunnel near the West Warszawa station and that 200,000 non-Jewish Poles were exterminated at the site.

Terror met with resistance from a significant number of Warsaw residents. The resistance varied in forms, from military style operations such as executions of high ranked military and police officers and large sabotage, to secret schools and small sabotage. The most famous act of resistance was the execution of "Warsaw's butcher", chief of police, SS general Franz Kutschera, who was responsible for the increase of roundups whose victims were either executed on the spot, sent to concentration camps or taken hostage to be shut in reprisal for civil disobedience or any attack on German soldiers. After Kutschera's death 300 hostages were killed in a public execution, but since then the high-ranking German officials realized that they are no longer safe or out of reach so, the number of roundups and executions significantly dropped.

Two days before the August 1, 1944 outbreak of the Warsaw Uprising two thousand men and the remaining 400 women of the Pawiak prison was sent to Gross-Rosen and Ravensbrück concentration camps. Subsequently the Polish insurgents captured the area but lost it to German forces. On August 21 the Germans shot an unknown number of remaining prisoners and burned and blew up the buildings.

THE WARSAW GHETTO UPRISING

INTRODUCTION

The Ghetto Uprising was an act of Jewish resistance to oppose Nazis' efforts to transport the remaining ghetto population to Majdanek and Treblinka concentration camps. After the "Grossaktion Warsaw" of summer 1942, in which more than a quarter of a million Jews were deported from the ghetto to Treblinka and murdered, the remaining Jews began to build bunkers and smuggle weapons and explosives into the ghetto. The left-wing Jewish Combat Organization (ŻOB) and right-wing Jewish Military Union (ŻZW) formed and began to train. The first resistance effort to another roundup in January 1943 was partially successful and spurred the Polish groups, from the other side of Ghetto wall, to provide greater support.

BACKGROUND

By the time Warsaw surrendered, ending the September campaign the number of Jews in and around the capital increased dramatically with thousands of refugees escaping the Polish-German front, often on foot. On October 12, 1939, the General Governorate (autonomous region of Germany) was established by Adolf Hitler in the occupied area of central Poland. The Nazi-appointed Jewish Council in Warsaw, a committee of 24 people headed by Adam Czerniaków, was responsible for carrying out German orders. On October 26, the Jews were mobilized as forced laborers to clear bomb damage and perform other hard labor. One month later, on November 20, the bank accounts of Polish Jews were blocked. On November 23, all Jewish establishments were ordered to display a Jewish star on doors and windows. Beginning December 1, all Jews older than ten (10) were compelled to wear a white armband, and on December 11, they

17

were forbidden from using public transit. On January 26, 1940, the Jews were banned from holding communal prayers due to "the risk of spreading epidemics." Food stamps were introduced by the German authorities, and measures were taken to liquidate all Jewish communities in the vicinity of Warsaw.

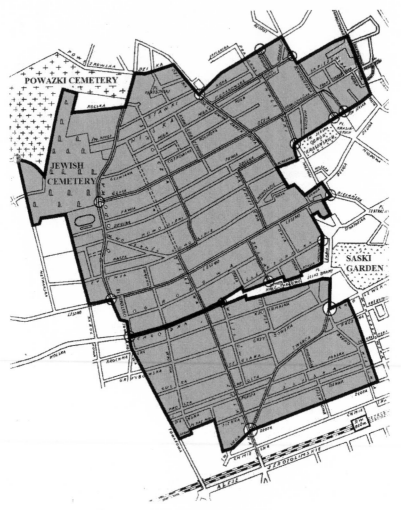

Plan of Ghetto - Source: Wikipedia – Black line – border wall,
Circles – entry points

On the orders of the Warsaw District Governor, Ludwig Fischer, the Ghetto wall construction started on April 1, 1940, circling the area of Warsaw inhabited predominantly by Jews. The work was supervised by the Warsaw Judenrat. The Nazi authorities expelled 113,000 ethnic Poles from the neighborhood and ordered the relocation of 138,000 Warsaw Jews from the suburbs into the city center. On October 16, 1940, the creation of the ghetto covering the area of 307 hectares (3.07 km2) was announced by the German Governor-General, Hans Frank. Before the Holocaust began, the number of Jews imprisoned there was between 375,000 and 400,000 (about 30% of the general population of the capital). The area of the ghetto constituted only about 2.4% of the overall metropolitan area.

The Germans closed the Warsaw Ghetto to the outside world on November 15, 1940. The wall around it was 3 m (9.8 ft) high and topped with barbed wire. Escapees were shot on sight. German policemen used to hold victory parties on the days when a large number of prisoners were shot at the ghetto fence.

The ghetto was divided in two along Chłodna Street, which was excluded from it, due to its local importance at that time (as one of Warsaw's east-west thoroughfares). The area southeast of Chłodna was known as the "Small Ghetto", while the area north of it became known as the "Large Ghetto". The two zones were connected at an intersection of Chłodna with Żelazna Street, where a special gate was built. In January 1942, the gate was removed, and a wooden footbridge was built over it, which became one of the postwar symbols of the Holocaust in occupied Poland.

The first walls around the ghetto began to be erected on April 1, 1940. Initially, the inhabitants of Warsaw were imprisoned there, who, according to racist Nuremberg laws were considered Jews. In the following months, people were brought to the ghetto from other towns of the pre-war Poland, areas annexed to the Third Reich (mainly from Łódź and the Ciechanów region), as well as other European countries. By March 1941, approximately 460,000 people lived there. The ghetto reached a population density of 146 thousand people per 1 km² - there were 3 people per room.

ws forcibly moved to Warsaw (Public Domain)

FAMINE

The huge, intentional, overpopulation caused tragic sanitary conditions, famine and the outbreak of infectious diseases. Famine was caused by reduction of food rations.

Based on their "scientific" calculations Nazis allocated different caloric targets for different ethnicities, corresponding with Nazi racial doctrine:

- Germans: >2000 cal. per day
- Ukrainians: 1000 cal. per day
- Poles: 600 cal. per day
- Jews: 180 cal. Per day

During the period from November 1940 to July 1942, about 100,000 people died of hunger and rampant disease and that was even before the mass deportations from the ghetto to the Treblinka extermination camp.

DEPORTATIONS

Between July 23 and September 21, 1942, the SS conducted a series of deportations as a part of the operation code-named Grossaktion Warschau (Great Action Warsaw). Just before the operation began, the German "Resettlement Commissioner" SS-Sturmbannführer Hermann Höfle called a meeting with the Ghetto Jewish Council, Judenrat, and informed its leader, Adam Czerniaków, that he would require 7,000 Jews a day for the "resettlement to the East". Failure would result in the execution of 100 hostages, including Council employees.

Realizing that deportation meant death, Czerniaków went to plead for the orphans. When he failed, he returned to his office and killed himself by taking a cyanide capsule. He left a suicide note to his wife, reading "They demand me to kill the children of my nation with my own hands. I have nothing to do but to die," and one to his fellow members of the Council, explaining: "I can no longer bear all this. My act will prove to everyone what is the right thing to do." He was succeeded by his deputy Marek Lichtenbaum. The population of the Ghetto was not informed about the real state of affairs and only by the end of 1942 did it become clear to them that the deportations, overseen by the Jewish Ghetto Police designated to supervise them, were to the Treblinka death camp and not for the purpose of resettlement.

"Selection" of Hungarian Jews on the ramp at Auschwitz-Birkenau

For eight weeks the rail shipments of Jews to Treblinka went on without stopping: 100 people to a cattle wagon, 5,000 to 6,000 each day including hospital patients and orphanage children. On arrival at Treblinka, stripped victims were marched to one of ten chambers disguised as showers and suffocated to death in batches of 200 with the use of monoxide gas. In September 1942, new gas chambers were built, which could kill as many as 3,000 people in just 2 hours.

Approximately 254,000–300,000 ghetto residents met their deaths at Treblinka during the two-month-long operation. The Grossaktion was directed by SS-Oberführer Ferdinand von Sammern-Frankenegg, the SS and police commander of the Warsaw area since 1941. He was relieved of duty by SS Polizeiführer Jürgen Stroop, sent to Warsaw by Heinrich Himmler on 17 April 1943. Stroop took over from von Sammern-Frankenegg following the failure of the latter to pacify the ghetto resistance.

JANUARY REVOLT

When the deportations first began, members of the Jewish resistance movement met and decided not to fight the SS directives, believing that the Jews were being sent to labor camps and not to their deaths. By the end of 1942, ghetto inhabitants learned that the deportations were part of an extermination process. Many of the remaining Jews decided to revolt.

S troops (Public Domain)

The first armed resistance in the ghetto occurred in January 1943. On January 18, the Germans began their second deportation of the Jews. While Jewish families hid in their so-called "bunkers", resistance fighters of both the ŻZW and the ŻOB, resisted, engaging the Germans in direct clashes. Though the they suffered heavy losses, the Germans also took casualties, and the deportation was halted within a few days. Only 5,000 Jews were deported, instead of the 8,000 planned. Hundreds of people in the Warsaw Ghetto were ready to fight, adults and children, sparsely armed with guns and gasoline bottles that had been smuggled into the ghetto by resistance fighters. Most of the Jewish fighters did not view their actions as an effective measure by which to save themselves, but rather as a battle for the honor of the Jewish people, and a protest the world's silence.

PREPARATIONS

Two resistance organizations, the ŻZW and ŻOB, took control of the ghetto. They built dozens of fighting posts and executed a number of Nazi collaborators, including Jewish Ghetto Police officers, members of the fake (German-sponsored and controlled) resistance organization Żagiew, as well as the Gestapo and Abwehr agents.

Żagiew (The Torch), also known as "Jewish Freedom Guard", was a Nazi-collaborationist Jewish agent-provocateur group, founded and sponsored by the Germans and led by Abraham Gancwajch. Many Żagiew members were related to the collaborationist Jewish organization Group 13, which was also led by Gancwajch. The organization operated primarily within the Warsaw Ghetto. Established in late 1940 it had over a thousand Jewish agents. Their prime goal was to infiltrate the Jewish resistance network and reveal its connections with the Polish underground that aided and hid Jews in the General Government. The organization was able to inflict considerable damage on both fronts. Żagiew agents were also instrumental in organizing the Hotel Polski affair, in Warsaw, a German scheme to lure thousands of wealthy Jews, under false promises of evacuation to South America, into a trap and extort their money and valuables before killing most of them.

The ŻOB established a prison to hold and execute traitors and collaborators. Józef Szeryński, former head of the Jewish Ghetto Police, committed suicide.

MAIN REVOLT

On 19 April 1943, on the eve of Passover, the police and SS auxiliary forces entered the ghetto. They were planning to complete the deportation action within three days but were ambushed by Jewish insurgents firing and tossing Molotov cocktails and hand grenades from alleyways, sewers, and windows. The Germans suffered 59 casualties and their advance bogged down. Two of their combat vehicles were set on fire by the insurgents' petrol bombs. The SS and police commander of Warsaw, von Sammern-Frankenegg's, for failure to contain the revolt was replaced by SS-Brigadeführer Jürgen Stroop, who rejected von Sammern-Frankenegg's proposal to call in bomber aircraft from Kraków and proceeded to lead a better-organized and reinforced ground attack.

When Stroop's ultimatum to surrender was rejected by the defenders, his forces resorted to systematically burn house block by block using flamethrowers and fire bottles and blowing up basements and sewers.

Burning Ghetto (Public Domain)

"We were beaten by the flames, not the Germans," said Marek Edelman, the last surviving leader of the Warsaw Ghetto Uprising. The "bunker wars" lasted an entire month, during which German progress was slowed.

While the battle continued inside the ghetto, Polish resistance groups engaged the Germans between 19 and 23 of April at six different locations outside the ghetto walls. In one attack, three AK units joined up in a failed attempt to breach the ghetto walls with explosives.

Eventually, the Jewish resistance group, ŻZW, lost all of its commanders and, on 29 April, the remaining fighters escaped the ghetto through the tunnel. The escape marked the end of significant fighting.

At this point, organized defense collapsed. Surviving fighters and thousands of remaining Jewish civilians took cover in the sewer system and in the many dugout hiding places hidden among the ruins of the ghetto, referred to as "bunkers" by Germans and Jews alike. The Germans used dogs to look for such hideouts, then usually dropped smoke bombs down to force people out. Sometimes they flooded these so-called bunkers or destroyed them with explosives.

On May 8, the Germans discovered a large "bunker" located at Miła 18 Street, which served as ŻOB's main command post. Most of the organization's remaining leadership and dozens of others committed mass suicide by ingesting cyanide, including the chief commander of ŻOB, Mordechaj Anielewicz. His deputy Marek Edelman escaped the ghetto through the sewers with a handful of comrades two days later.

The suppression of the uprising officially ended on 16 May 1943, when Stroop personally pushed a detonator button to demolish the Great Synagogue of Warsaw.

Sporadic resistance continued and the last skirmish took place on 5 June 1943 between the Germans and a holdout group of armed Jews without connections to the resistance organizations.

Captured Jews are led to the assembly point for deportation (Public Domain)

13,000 Jews were killed in the ghetto during the uprising (some 6,000 among them were burnt alive or died from smoke inhalation). Of the remaining 50,000 residents, almost all were captured and shipped to Majdanek and Treblinka.

German casualties were probably less than 150, with Stroop reporting only 110 casualties (17 dead, 93 wounded).

After the uprising was over, most of the incinerated houses were razed, and the Warsaw concentration camp complex was established in their place.

OUTSIDE HELP

Due to the nature of the conflict and that it took place within the confines of the German-guarded Warsaw Ghetto, the role of the Polish Home Army was primarily one of ancillary support; namely, the provision of arms, ammunition and training. Although the Home Army's stocks were meager, and general provision of arms limited, the right-wing ŻZW received from them significant quantities of armaments, including some heavy and light machine guns, submachine guns, rifles, pistols and grenades.

The Polish Home Army also disseminated information and appeals to help the Jews in the ghetto, both in Poland and by way of radio transmissions to the Allies, which fell largely on deaf ears. During the uprising, the Polish Resistance units of the Polish Home Army and the communist People's Guard attacked German units near the ghetto walls and attempted to smuggle weapons, ammunition, supplies, and instructions into the ghetto. The failure to break through the German defenses, limited supplies to the ghetto, which was otherwise cut off from the outside world by a German blockade.

It was the largest single revolt by Jews during World War II. The Jews knew that the uprising was doomed, and their survival was unlikely. Marek Edelman, the only surviving commander, said that the motivation for fighting was "to pick the time and place of our deaths".

After 5 years of brutal German occupation on August 1, 1944 there were 900,000 people in Warsaw.

WARSAW UPRISING
BACKGROUND

In 1944, Poland had been occupied by Nazi Germany for almost five years. The Polish Home Army since its inception in 1942, created from the "Armed Resistance" and other smaller groups of Polish underground forces, planned a large nationwide uprising against German forces.

Home Army soldiers (IPN.gov.pl)

The initial goal of the Home Army was not only to unite all of the resistance forces, but to actually transform into the regular army at the end of the uprising that would cooperate with the Allies as they liberated Europe from the Nazis. The army would be 400,000 strong.

When the Soviet Army began its offensive in 1943, it became clear that Poland would be "liberated" by the Soviets instead of the Western Allies. The Soviets and the Poles had a common enemy, Germany, but there was no trust between them. Both sides remembered the Polish-Soviet war of 1920 and Russians already showed their desire to exact their revenge for the loss on those who served in the Polish army at the time. Poles were aware of the fact that in the "second lines" of the "liberating" Red Army were the NKVD, the predecessor of the KGB, henchmen with the lists, compiled by local Communist activists, of those that had to be dealt with.

For Polish leaders it was obvious that the advancing Soviet Red Army might not come to Poland as an ally, but rather as "the ally of an ally".

The Soviet partisans in Poland often clashed with a Polish resistance united under the Home Army. Stalin broke off Polish-Soviet relations in April 1943, after the Germans revealed the Katyn massacre of Polish army officers and refused to admit to ordering the killings and denounced the claims as German propaganda. The Western alliance accepted Stalin's words as truth in order to keep the Anti-Nazi alliance intact. In October, the Polish government-in-exile issued instructions to the effect that if diplomatic relations with the Soviet Union were not resumed before the Soviet entry into Poland, Home Army forces were to remain underground pending further decisions.

On November 20th, 1943 the commander of the Home Army, Tadeusz Bór-Komorowski, outlined a plan, which became known as Operation Tempest. On the approach of the Eastern Front, local units of the Home Army were to harass the German Wehrmacht in the rear and co-operate with incoming Soviet units as much as possible. General Bór-Komorowski was authorized by the government in exile to proclaim a general uprising whenever he saw fit.

HOME ARMY

The Home Army (AK - for Armia Krajowa) was the dominant Polish resistance movement in Poland during World War II. (Interestingly enough, no other military unit in the World used such a name, ever.) The AK was formed in February 1942 from the units of Union of Armed Struggle. Over the next two years, AK absorbed most other Polish underground forces. Its allegiance was to the Polish government-in-exile, and it was considered an armed wing of what became known as the "Polish Underground State".

(From this point, as a tribute to the soldiers of Home Army/Armia Krajowa I will use the acronym AK that they used for their name throughout their struggle.)

AK soldiers during Warsaw Uprising (Public Domain)

Estimates of the AK's strength in 1944 range from 200,000 to 600,000, the most commonly cited number being 400,000. This last number would make the AK not only the largest Polish underground resistance movement, but one of the largest in Europe during World War II. The AK was disbanded on 19 January 1945, after the Soviet Red Army had largely cleared Polish territory of German forces.

The AK sabotaged German operations such as transports headed for the Eastern Front in the Soviet Union. It also fought several full-scale battles against the Germans, particularly in 1943 and in Operation Tempest in 1944. The AK tied down substantial German forces and destroyed much-needed German supplies.

The partisans also defended Polish civilians against atrocities perpetrated by other military formations.

Because the AK was loyal to the Polish Government-in-Exile, the Soviet Union saw it as an obstacle to Communism in Poland. Consequently, over the course of the war, conflict grew between the AK and Soviet forces. During the Soviet occupation of Poland, thousands of former AK operatives were deported to Gulags and Soviet prisons, while others - including senior commanders like Leopold Okulicki and Emil August Fieldorf - were executed.

AK's numbers in 1944 include a cadre of over 10,000–11,000 officers, 7,500 officers-in-training and 88,000 non-commissioned officers (NCOs). The officer cadre was formed from pre-war officers and NCOs, graduates of underground courses, and elite operatives usually parachuted in from the West.

It is believed that during the Uprising 30%, around 12,000, of AK soldiers were women, but at the end of the fighting only 2,500 were taken prisoner.

Among the AK's rank were also young boys between 11 and 18 years old. It is very difficult to determine their number, but again, at the end of the fighting 1,100 of them became POWs.

To this day, every Polish child knows what the acronym AK stands for.

GRAY RANKS

Polish youth played a major role in the uprising, among them were Polish scouts, members of Gray Ranks.

"Gray Ranks" was a code name for the underground paramilitary scouting organization. Created on September 27, 1939, it actively resisted and fought the German occupation in Warsaw and contributed to the resistance operations of the Polish Underground State. Some of its members, Assault Groups, were among the Home Army's best-trained troops.

ray Ranks soldiers 1 month into Uprising (Public Domain)

Though formally independent, the Gray Ranks worked closely with the Home Army Headquarters. They had their own headquarters known under the cryptonym "Bee Yard" staffed by the Chief Scout plus three to five deputies in the rank of the Scoutmaster.

Since 1916, scouts within the Polish Scouting and Guiding Association (ZHP) had taken an active part in all the conflicts Poland was engaged in around this time: Greater Poland Uprising, Polish-Bolshevik War, Silesian Uprisings, and the Polish–Ukrainian War. After the German invasion of Poland in 1939, the Nazis recognized the ZHP as a threat. Polish Scouts and Guides were branded as criminals and banned.

Under the leadership of Florian Marciniak, the ZHP carried on as a clandestine organization. The wartime Scouts evolved into the paramilitary Gray Ranks, reporting to the Underground State.

The name Gray Ranks (Szare Szeregi) was adopted in 1940. Originally, it was used by underground scouts in Poznań. The name was coined after an early action of the ZHP, in which boy scouts distributed propaganda leaflets among Germans from Lithuania, Latvia and Estonia who had settled in the homes of expelled Poles. To create confusion, the leaflets had been signed SS for Szare Szeregi (Gray Ranks), but also used by major German paramilitary organization, SS.

Girl-guide postmen during the Warsaw Uprising (Public Domain)

Older Scouts carried out sabotage, armed resistance, and assassinations. The Girl Guides formed auxiliary units working as nurses, liaisons and munition carriers. Younger Scouts were involved in so-called minor sabotage which included dropping leaflets or painting the "Kotwica" sign (resembling an anchor) on the walls. The Gray Ranks units fighting in Warsaw uprising were among the most effective ones in combat.

The Gray Ranks followed the prewar principles of the Polish Scouting Association: service to the people and country, education and improvement of skills. In addition to the prewar oath, the following line was added:
"I pledge to you that I shall serve in the Gray Ranks, safeguard the secrets of the organization, obey orders, and not hesitate to sacrifice my life."

In addition to the Scouting moral code, the Gray Ranks also followed a basic three-step path of action. The program was nicknamed "Today - tomorrow - the day after":

"Today" – struggle for Poland's independence

"Tomorrow" – prepare for an all-national uprising and the liberation of Poland

"The Day After" – prepare to rebuild Poland after the war

As of May 1, 1944, the Gray Ranks numbered 8,359 members. Their structure was as follows:

Zawiszacy (plural of Zawisza) - the younger Scouts.

Troops organized for children between 12 and 14 years of age named after Zawisza Czarny, a medieval Polish knight. The troops did not take part in active resistance. Instead, the children were prepared for auxiliary service for the upcoming all-national uprising and taught in secret schools for their future duties in liberated Poland. Among the best-known auxiliary troops formed by the young scouts was the Scouting Postal Service.

Postmen (Public Domain)

The idea of the postal service came from the Polish scouts who saw the problems facing civilians and their need to communicate with separated family members. It was launched on August 6, 1944 and in just a few days its network covered the entire city. It had 8 offices and 40 mailboxes located in various parts of the city. During the 63 days of uprising 200,000 pieces of mail, or simply messages, were delivered.

Combat Schools - youth aged 15 to 17.

They took part in "minor sabotage" operations. These included propaganda operations directed at the Poles, German civilians and German military units. The best-known operations were:

- Operation Wawer-Palmiry – a major propaganda campaign, which included painting patriotic and anti-German slogans on walls; distribution of leaflets, posters, and fake issues of supposed German newspapers; intercepting German propaganda megaphones and using them to spread Polish propaganda; destroying German flags and other symbols; disrupting German events by setting off fire alarms; and, last but not least, stink-bombing German-operated movie theaters.

- Operation N - the distribution of propaganda newspapers and leaflets among German soldiers stationed in Poland.

- Operation WISS - an operation on behalf of Home Army intelligence, in which Combat School groups carried out surveillance of German military units and their movements. The information that was gathered was passed on to the Allies. The operation provided the Allies with complete lists of German units, their insignia and approximate complements, including units down to battalion size.

As part of their secret training, the Combat Schools boys and girls prepared for service with the Home Army as members of commanders' troops, communication units, and reconnaissance units. During the Warsaw Uprising, Combat School units in Warsaw's Downtown District formed a company; in other districts, they formed platoons.

Assault Groups - comprising youngsters aged 17 and up.

They were directly subordinate to the Home Army's KeDyw (Directorate of Diversion). The groups trained at secret NCO and officer schools. Most members also studied at underground universities, to gain knowledge necessary to reconstruct Poland after the war.

The Assault Groups took part in "major sabotage", as well as armed engagements. The assault groups formed the backbone of the Home Army's special troops. They liberated prisoners from German prisons and transports, blew up railroad bridges, carried out executions ordered by special courts, and fought pitched battles against German forces.

Paramedic (Public Domain)

The Assault Groups in Warsaw were organized into several battalions, including "Baszta", "Zośka", "Parasol" and "Wigry", which later took part in the Warsaw Uprising and were among the most notable and successful units on the Polish side.

Notable assault-group operations included:

- Operation Arsenal (March 26, 1943), the liberation of the gravely wounded Jan Bytnar and 24 other prisoners from a Gestapo convoy
- Operation Schultz (May 6, 1943), the assassination of SS-Obersturmführer Herbert Schultz;
- Operation Lange (May 22, 1943), the assassination of SS-Rottenführer Ewald Lange;
- Operation Belt (August 1943 – February 1944), the destruction of thirteen German border outposts;
- Operation Bürkl (September 7, 1943), the assassination of SS-Oberscharführer Franz Bürkl;
- Operation Kutschera (February 2, 1944), the assassination of SS and Police Leader Franz Kutschera;
- Storming and liberation of Gęsiówka concentration camp in Warsaw on August 5, 1944.

Paramedics

The bravest of them all were the women partisans.

(The girl in the picture on the previous page was probably the youngest among the paramedics, +/-8 years old, she was one of the few who survived.)

They represented 22 percent of the fighters (+/- 10K) of the Warsaw Uprising. Their main roles were as paramedics, and couriers, but many of them also fought on the front lines. The paramedics and couriers did not have weapons, only their wits and street smart.

The paramedics went into action with their units. When one of the soldiers was wounded, they had to pull him to a safer place, dress the wound, lead him, drag him or carry him on a stretcher to a dressing point. In case of serious wounds, arrange transport to the hospital. Because they were under fire, they often got wounded themselves. Headbands with a red cross did not protect the nurses from bullets. Quite the opposite - for the Germans, they were an easy target. They had no qualms about shooting at unarmed women, dropping bombs on hospitals, and murdering patients and doctors there.

Paramedics patrol (Public Domain)

WEAPONS

The lack of equipment forced the resistance to produce their own in clandestine conditions, right under the Germans' noses. This list contains four essential weapons originally (mass) produced by the AK.

"Błyskawica" submachine gun
The Błyskawica (lightning), was a submachine gun produced by the AK in occupied Poland. Together with a Polish version of the Sten submachine gun, with which it shares some design elements, it was the only weapon mass-produced covertly in occupied Europe during World War II.

AK soldier holding a Blyskawica gun (Public Domain)

In 1942 engineer Wacław Zawrotny proposed to the AK command that he and his colleagues prepare a project of a cheap, home-made machine pistol for use by the Polish resistance. Its main feature was its simplicity, so that the weapon could be made even in small workshops, by inexperienced engineers. The idea was accepted, and Zawrotny, together with his colleague Seweryn Wielanier, prepared a project of a sub-machine gun, soon afterward named Błyskawica. To allow for easier production, all parts of the weapon were joined together with screws and threads rather than bolts and welding.

The design was based on two of the most popular submachine guns of the era. The external construction with a retractable butt and magazine mounted under the gun was borrowed from the successful German MP 40. The internal design of the mechanism was modeled after the British Sten, Blowback, with an open bolt. It offered good performance and high reliability. The weapon was designed in such a fashion that resistance army members could use any captured stocks of German MP40 ammunition cartridges.

The production started in a workshop officially producing metal fence nets in Warsaw. Until 1944 and the start of Operation Tempest roughly 600 pieces were built in Warsaw. During the Warsaw Uprising an additional 40 were built.

"Filipinka" hand grenade

"Filipinka" was a commonly used name for the AK during World War II in occupied Poland. It was designed by a former worker of the Rembertów Polish Army munition works, Edward Tymoszak. It was partially based on his pre-war design of an anti-tank grenade.

The Filipinka was an offensive impact grenade, cylindrical in shape. The filling was composed mostly of homemade explosives, explosives from German air bombs and artillery shells, as well as British plastic explosive delivered by air drops.

The coating was painted with various colors to allow for easier usage in resistance service and easier hiding. Throughout the war approximately 240,000 grenades of this type were produced.

Sidolówka hand grenade

Sidolówka was a common fragmentation hand grenade, produced by the AK.

The name of the grenade came from Sidol, a metal-cleaning agent from Henkel sold in Poland at the time. The first grenades used the Sidol bottles as the casing. Later on the casing was purposely modelled after the bottle in order to allow for easier hiding of the weapon.

Sidolówka was first produced in Warsaw in 1942, by the professors of the Warsaw University of Technology under the leadership of Jan Czochralski. It was partially based on an earlier design of the Filipinka grenade.

It was a fragmentation grenade with a 4.5 second delay time. It is estimated that until the end of World War II, 350,000 grenades were produced in Polish underground factories.

The K pattern flamethrower

The K pattern flamethrower was a man-portable backpack flamethrower, produced in occupied Poland during World War II for the AK.

Design work upon a simple flamethrower for the Polish underground, suitable for clandestine production in ordinary workshops, of readily available materials, started in 1942 on request of the AK headquarters. Its main purpose was to be used against armored vehicles.

The K-pattern flame thrower appeared a successful weapon, considering its primitive design and conditions of manufacturing. Its main flaw was that the air pressure decreased during operation, and so successive bursts had a progressively shorter range. The weapon could be re-fueled by fuel carriers and a procedure took about 4 minutes.

AK's Flamethrower (Public Domain)

At the outbreak of the Warsaw Uprising the Polish forces had only 30 flamethrowers (many had been lost in stores either captured by the Germans or out of reach). Nonetheless, they were actively used in sectors of most fierce street fighting during the uprising.

Kubuś, the Armored Car

Kubuś (Polish for "Little Jacob") was an improvised fighting vehicle used in the early stages of the uprising. It was built on a chassis of a Chevrolet 157 truck, and it took part in the Warsaw battles. It was originally produced within 13 days and handed out to fighters without previous testing. The designer constructed the chassis without previous plans on paper and installed it on site. The chassis was mounted on the base with steel plates for protection of the crew. The car could carry between eight and twelve soldiers. It was armed with a Soviet DP machine gun and a K pattern flamethrower.

Kubuś suffered damage and was abandoned after two weeks of service.

Kubuś (Public Domain)

VIS pistol

VIS model 35 (wz. 35) is a 9×19mm caliber, single-action, semi-automatic pistol. Its design was inspired by American firearms inventor John Browning's 9mm "Browning GP".

Production of the VIS began at the Fabryka Broni arms factory in 1935 and was adopted as the standard handgun of the Polish Army the following year. The pistol was valued by the Germans and towards the end of the war issued to German paratroopers. Largely based on the Browning Hi-Power and using 9 mm rounds, the Vis is highly prized among collectors of firearms.

GERMANS

In late July 1944 the German units stationed in and around Warsaw were divided into three categories.

The first and the most numerous was the garrison of Warsaw. As of 31 July, it numbered some 11,000 troops under General Rainer Stahel. These well-equipped German forces prepared for the defense of the city's key positions for many months. Several hundred concrete bunkers and barbed wire lines protected the buildings and areas occupied by the Germans. Apart from the garrison itself, numerous army units were stationed on both banks of the Vistula and in the city.

The second category was formed by police and SS under Col. Paul Otto Geibel, numbering initially 5,710 men, including Schutzpolizei and Waffen-SS.

The third category was formed by various auxiliary units, including detachments of the Bahnschutz (rail guard), Werkschutz (factory guard), the Polish Volksdeutsche (ethnic Germans in Poland) and paramilitary units.

German officer (Public Domain)

During the uprising the German side received reinforcements on a daily basis. General Stahel was replaced as overall commander by SS-General Erich von dem Bach in early August. As of August 20, 1944, the German units directly involved with fighting in Warsaw comprised 17,000 men arranged in two battle groups: Battle Group Rohr (commanded by Major General Rohr), which included 1,700 soldiers of the anti-communist S.S. Sturmbrigade R.O.N.A. (Russian National Liberation Army, also known as Kaminski Brigade) under German command made up of Russian, Belorussian and Ukrainian collaborators, and Battle Group Reinefarth commanded by SS-Gruppenführer Heinz Reinefarth, which consisted of Attack Group Dirlewanger (commanded by Oskar Dirlewanger), which included Aserbaidschanische Legion, Attack Group Reck (commanded by Major Reck), Attack Group Schmidt (commanded by Colonel Schmidt) and various support and backup units. The Nazi forces included about 5,000 regular troops; 4,000 Luftwaffe personnel; as well as about 2,000 men of the Sentry Regiment Warsaw, including four infantry battalions, and an SS reconnaissance squadron with 350 men.

Altogether, initially there were 25,000 troops, but throughout the course of the uprising the number rose to 50,000.

EVE OF THE BATTLE

On July 13, 1944 the Soviet offensive crossed the old Polish border. At this point the Poles had to make a decision: either initiate the uprising that would be seen as an attempt to preemptively capture the government and political influence and risk a lack of Soviet support, or fail to rebel and face Soviet propaganda describing the Home Army as Nazi collaborators. They feared that if Poland was liberated by the Red Army, then the Allies would ignore the London-based Polish government in the aftermath of the war. On July 21, the High Command of the Home Army decided that the time to launch Operation Tempest in Warsaw was imminent. On July 25, the Polish government-in-exile, without the knowledge of Polish Commander-in-Chief General Kazimierz Sosnkowski, approved the plan for an uprising in Warsaw leaving the exact time and date to the local commander.

On July 27, the German Governor of the Warsaw District, Ludwig Fischer, issued an order for 100,000 Polish men and women to report for work on fortifications around the city to stop advancing Soviet troops. The Germans intended to keep the Warsaw at all costs and therefore were converting it into the fortress. The inhabitants of Warsaw ignored this order, and the Home Army command became worried about possible reprisals, defiance was punishable by death, or mass roundups. The Soviet forces were approaching Warsaw, and Soviet-controlled radio stations called for the Polish people to rise in arms.

On July 29, the (Communist) Union of Polish Patriots, in a broadcast from Moscow, called on the Poles "thirsting to fight" rise up against the Germans "to smash the foe before he can recover from his defeat".

On 29 July, the first Soviet armored units reached the outskirts of Warsaw, where they were counterattacked by two German Panzer Corps: the 39th and 4th SS. On 29 July 1944 Radio Station Kosciuszko located in Moscow transmitted several appeals "to Warsaw" and called "Fight the Germans!".

Believing that the time for action had arrived, on July 31st, the Polish commanders, General Bór-Komorowski and Colonel Antoni Chruściel, ordered the full mobilization of the underground forces for 17:00 the following day.

THE "W" HOUR

The Polish commanders scheduled the beginning of the uprising, the "W" hour (*), for 5:00 pm on August 1st.

Some people ask why 5 o'clock in the afternoon and not early morning that would give them the element of surprise? Warsaw at the time had a Police curfew when any civilians could have been, and often were, shot on sight. Moving groups of young people around the city to their assembly points was simply impossible. It was easier to conceal them in broad daylight among others doing their daily routines. It was not an ideal solution and the movement of people was eventually detected and resulted in the early skirmishes in three different locations. The detection was also a result of anticipation of such revolt by Germans. What they did not realize was the size and strength of it.

At 4:30 p.m. the Governor of Warsaw put the military garrison on full alert.

Despite all that difficulties that evening the poorly armed resistance, of 40,000 fighters only 2,500 were armed, captured a major arsenal, the main post office, the power station and the tallest building in Warsaw (2nd tallest in Europe), the Prudential building. In the following days the resistance fighters were most successful in the City Centre, Old Town, and Wola districts. However, several major strongholds including the police district and the airport remained in German hands. In some areas of Wola district the Poles sustained heavy losses that forced an early retreat. In other areas such as Mokotów, the attackers controlled only the residential areas. Most crucially, the fighters in different areas failed to link up with each other and with areas outside Warsaw, leaving each sector isolated from the others. After the first hours of fighting, many units had to switch to a defensive strategy and the barricades started to be built.

"My Führer, the timing is unfortunate, but from a historical perspective, what the Poles are doing is a blessing. After five, six weeks we shall leave. But by then Warsaw, the capital, the head, the intelligence of this former 16–17 million Polish people will be extinguished, this Volk that has blocked our way to the east for seven hundred years and has stood in our way ever since the First Battle of Tannenberg. After this the Polish problem will no longer be a great historical problem for the children who come after us, nor indeed will it be for us." - SS Chief Heinrich Himmler to Adolf Hitler when he learned about the Warsaw Uprising.

On 1 August 1944 Hitler and Himmler released their "Order for Warsaw", which stands as one of the most barbaric documents of the war: *"Every citizen of Warsaw is to be killed, including men, women and children,... Warsaw has to be levelled to the ground in order to set a terrifying example to the rest of Europe."*

* "W" stands for "wybuch powstania" or "uprising explosion".

FIRST FOUR DAYS

Hitler's first reaction to the news of the uprising was to issue an order to start the air raids on Warsaw. The German Luftwaffe was to use all planes of the "central front" to "level Warsaw to the ground" and suppress the uprising. However, it soon turned out that it was impossible. In the city, a number of German offices and military and police units were cut off and surrounded. In this situation, the task of organizing the relief for Warsaw garrison Hitler entrusted to Heinrich Himmler and general Heinz Guderian.

As originally planned the uprising was to last only a few days, until the Russian army arrived. As such all important advances made by the resistance were made in the first four days. Here is what happened in those few days:

• The city center and the Old Town: Polish units captured most of their assigned territory, but failed to capture areas with strong pockets of resistance from the Germans: the Warsaw University buildings, phone company (PAST) skyscraper, the headquarters of the German garrison, the German-only sector, and the bridges over the Vistula. They thus failed to create a central stronghold, secure communication links to other areas, or a secure land connection with the northern area of the Zoliborz district through the northern railway line and the Citadel.

• Districts of Żoliborz, Marymont and Bielany: Units failed to secure the most important military targets near Żoliborz. Many units retreated outside of the city, into the forests. Although they captured most of the area around Żoliborz they failed to secure the Citadel area and break through the German defenses at Warsaw - Gdańsk railway station.

First few days (Public Domain)

- District of Wola: Units initially secured most of the territory but sustained heavy losses (up to 30%). Some units retreated into the forests, while others retreated to the eastern part of the area. In the northern part of Wola the soldiers of Colonel Jan Mazurkiewicz managed to capture the German barracks, the German supply depot, and the flanking position at the Okopowa Jewish Cemetery.

- District of Ochota: The units mobilized in this area did not capture either the territory or the military targets (the Gęsiówka concentration camp or the SS and Sipo barracks). After suffering heavy casualties, most of the Home Army forces retreated to the forests west of Warsaw. Only two small units of approximately 200 to 300 men under Lieut. Chyczewski remained in the area and managed to create strong pockets of resistance. They were later reinforced by units from the downtown. Elite units of the Kedyw managed to secure most of the northern part of the area and captured all of the military targets there. However, they were soon tied down by German tactical counterattack from the south and west.

- District of Mokotow: The situation in this area was very serious from the start of hostilities. The partisans planned to capture the heavily

48

defended Police Sector, and establish a connection with the downtown through open terrain at the former airfield of Mokotów Field. As both of the areas were heavily fortified and could be approached only through open terrain, the assaults failed. Some units retreated into the forests, while others managed to capture parts of Lower Mokotow, which was, however, cut off from most communication routes.

● District of Praga: The Uprising was also started on the right bank of the Vistula, where the main task was to seize the bridges over the river and secure the bridgeheads until the arrival of the Red Army. It was clear that, since the location was far worse than that of the other areas, there was no chance of any help from outside. After some minor initial successes, the forces of Lt. Col. Antoni Żurowski were badly outnumbered by the Germans. The Home Army forces were forced to retreat.

● City suburbs: this area consisted of territories outside Warsaw city limits. Partisans mostly failed to capture their targets.

On the 4th day of the uprising, the German army stopped its retreat westwards and began receiving reinforcements. On the same day SS General Erich von dem Bach was appointed commander of all the forces employed against the Uprising. From that point on the German counter attacks aimed to link up with the remaining German pockets and then cut off the Uprising from the Vistula river.

RUSSIA'S REACTION TO THE UPRISING

"Despite broadcasting messages in late July 1944 encouraging Warsaw residents to rise up against the German occupiers, Soviet forces did not stir to help them. Though the Red Army was positioned right across the Vistula River outside Warsaw and could have intervened, Stalin was happy to let the Germans slaughter the Polish Home Army." - Sean McMeekin, The Wall Street Journal, July 31, 2019.

Russian and Polish troops enter Praga district (right side of the river) (Public Domain)

Soviet propaganda claimed that the Red Army was not able to provide effective assistance to the uprising, because after intense battles in Belarus, its units were tired and too far away from the supply bases. There were also claims that the uprising was not agreed upon with the Soviet command and that the Polish capital did not play a major role in the Soviet war plans anyway.

However, the documents revealed after the collapse of the USSR contradict those claims. They show that the Soviet 2nd Armored Army, which led a direct attack in the direction of Warsaw, was introduced in the first line on July 22, and its supply bases were about 300 kilometers away. 2nd Army had three times more supplies of ammunition and fuel than the Soviet 69th Army fighting nearby.

On July 28, 1944 an order was issued for the First Belarusian Front to attack Warsaw with its right wing, and no later than August 5-8 capture Warsaw's district Praga (separated from Warsaw by the Vistula river) and cross the Vistula by Pułtusk and Serock.

This document shows that the Soviet command planned to capture Warsaw in the first days of August 1944. At the same time, Soviet propaganda, by means of radio broadcasts and dropping of leaflets, called on the inhabitants of Warsaw to fight with the Germans. There are many indications that Stalin planned to quickly acquire the Polish capital, and moreover, for political reasons, he paid a lot of attention to it, as he intended to locate there a newly established Polish Committee of National Liberation.

The defeat in the tank battle near Warsaw slowed down the Red Army's attack, but to a lesser extent than it was later presented by Soviet propaganda. Documents stored in the Central Archives of the Ministry of Defense of the Russian Federation (dated July 1944) do not mention the collapse of the attack on Warsaw due to German resistance. It is true that on August 1st the commanding officer of the armored army, General Radziejewski, gave his troops an order to take a defensive posture, but it was supposed to be only a tactical break - necessary to supplement the supplies of ammunition and fuel. On August 2, the Soviet "Pravda" cheered the Red Army soldiers with the slogan "to Warsaw!". The Soviet advantage was clear at the time and in all likelihood the Germans would not be able to keep the city.

Reports submitted by the Soviet front troops showed that at the beginning of August 1944, the west bank of the Vistula was in many places unmanned by the Germans. The command of the German 9th Army assessed the situation in the Warsaw region as catastrophic. The outbreak of the Warsaw Uprising surprised Stalin. Because of that the attitude of the Soviets was initially ambivalent.

Moscow tried to hide the uprising from its own people. In the reports of the First Belarussian Front from August and the first half of September, there is no mention of battles in Warsaw. Also, the comments of the Soviet press were initially few and cautious.

THE ATTITUDE OF THE U.S. AND BRITAIN TOWARDS THE UPRISING

The date of the uprising was not agreed with the Western Allies - but they could not claim that they were completely surprised by its outbreak. On July 27, 1944, the Polish ambassador in London, Edward Raczyński, met with the Minister of Foreign Affairs of the United Kingdom, Anthony Eden, where he asked the British to:

1. Send the Polish 1st Independent Parachute Brigade to the Polish capital,
2. Give the Polish Home Army four Polish air squadrons,
3. Bomb the German airports near Warsaw,
4. Recognize the veterans' rights of the Home Army soldiers.

Eden promised to consider these demands urgently but questioned the technical feasibility of implementing them. The next day the Foreign Office officially informed Raczyński that it is impossible to meet Polish demands. On the news of the outbreak of the uprising, Ambassador Raczyński went to the British Ministry of Foreign Affairs, where he asked the Under Secretary of State Alexander Cadogan to immediately inform Prime Minister Churchill about the Warsaw uprising and to issue orders enabling the commencement of discharges of weapons and ammunition for AK units.

The "Big Three" at the Tehran Conference (Public Domain)

On August 3, President Władysław Raczkiewicz approached Churchill with a request for immediate airlift of weapons and ammunition to Warsaw. A similar appeal to the British military authorities was made by generals

Kukiel and Kopański. Three days later Jan Ciechanowski, the Polish ambassador in Washington, submitted to the American College of Joint Chiefs of Staff a formal request of the Polish government to organize help for the uprising. The diplomatic action aimed at organizing effective support for the insurgents has since been intensively conducted by all the agencies of the Polish government in exile.

The first Allied reactions were cautious and reluctant. The Americans declared that the support for the Polish underground is under the authority of the British government, and due to the fact that Warsaw lies in the Soviet operational zone, the Allies will not be able to conduct any operations there without Moscow's consent. In turn, General Hastings Ismay - chief military adviser to Churchill - after a five-day delay declared that the use of RAF bombers in Poland can be considered only in conjunction with the expected actions of the Red Army and considered the remaining Polish postulates of a military nature as unrealistic. On August 16, Polish generals met with Colonel Harold B. Perkins - the head of the Polish and Czechoslovak SOE faculties. During the conversation, the Briton blamed the Poles for the situation in Warsaw and stated that "it is a crime to plan help for Warsaw as part of operations as risky as those currently being undertaken". Negative attitude was also presented by the British Foreign Ministry. Minister Eden blocked a proposal that, in response to the mass crimes committed by the Germans in Warsaw, an extraordinary session of the House of Commons should be called to discuss the retaliatory bombardment of Berlin. The Allies also delayed the granting of veteran rights to AK soldiers, claiming that they would only be able to do so if the USSR did likewise. It was not until 30 August that the governments of the United States and the United Kingdom officially declared that they would recognize the Home Army as an integral part of the Polish Armed Forces. The obstruction and reluctance of the British military and administrative structures was contrasted with the personal attitude of Prime Minister Churchill, who already on August 3 ordered immediate preparations of flights with supplies to Warsaw and pressed the RAF command to give the insurgents all possible help.

On August 4, the British Prime Minister also sent a first message to Stalin informing about the outbreak of the uprising and planned allied help. In the following days, numerous requests for support for the uprising were sent to the Soviet side by the British military mission and the embassy in Moscow. On August 12, Churchill again wired to Stalin asking for help for the fighting Warsaw, but he received a refused response in a sharp tone. When Moscow did not agree to the landing of Allied airplanes at Soviet airports, Churchill decided to involve President Roosevelt in this matter. The American administration, however, was reluctant to think about straining relations with the USSR. It was not until August 20 that Churchill and Roosevelt sent a joint letter to Stalin, which included the words: "We wonder what the reaction of world public opinion will be if the anti-fascists in Warsaw are actually abandoned. We believe that all three of us should do everything we can to save as many patriots as possible." This letter - deliberately outlined by Roosevelt in a gentle tone - ended with the statement that "the time factor is extremely important". After Stalin's unusually brutal response, Roosevelt took a clear course to avoid confrontation. When Churchill offered to send him a sharper note, the American president refused to take a stand for several days ("I do not know what further steps we could take now") to finally refuse ("I consider unfavorable for the further course of the general war to join the proposed dispatch"). On September 5, Admiral William D. Leahy erroneously informed Roosevelt that the uprising in Warsaw had collapsed, which the latter treated as a pretext to make the matter of putting pressure on Stalin to be outdated.

It seems that the Warsaw Uprising - just as the Katyn massacre - was an obstacle for the diplomatic relations among the Great Three. For Roosevelt and his administration, Poland was not a full-fledged partner, but a small ally which was making cooperation with the USSR more difficult. There was a very small interest of the American administration in the events in Warsaw, and knowledge about the situation in Poland was very limited.

Prime Minister Churchill seemed to be honestly taken by the tragedy of Warsaw and tried to give the greatest possible help to the uprising, however, as the weakest member of the "Big Three" he had no opportunity to do so. Even he was not prepared to break cooperation with the USSR because of Poland. Churchill's memoirs published after the war show that the members of the British government were seriously outraged by the USSR's attitude to the uprising, but the Soviet authorities were pushing back strongly because, as the British prime minister explained, 'we must remember the fate of millions of people fighting on all fronts "and the" main goal sometimes requires even humiliating submission'. The British press during the uprising presented little interest in events in Warsaw. In particular, the left-wing newspapers tried to justify the attitude of the USSR and presented a clearly negative attitude towards the leaders of the Home Army and the Polish government in exile. The editor of the Polish section of the BBC, Gregory MacDonald, was forced to admit that the information about the lack of Soviet assistance for the uprising was significantly toned down so as not to fuel the atmosphere of emotions and not overstep the need for allied unity". On October 5, Churchill in his speech in the House of Commons declared that the epic of Warsaw would not be forgotten.

According to historians, research into the lack of support of the Warsaw Uprising is very difficult due to lack of access to archives. For records relating to the period, currently both the United Kingdom archives and Russian archives remain mostly closed to the public. Further complicating the matter is, the United Kingdom's claim that they accidentally destroyed the archives of the Polish Government in Exile.

THE WOLA MASSACRE

On August 5, three German battle groups made out of the Wehrmacht, the SS Police, the SS-Sturmbrigade RONA and the SS-Sturmbrigade Dirlewanger, an infamous Waffen SS penal unit led by Oskar Dirlewanger, started their advance toward the city center from the western outskirts of the Wola district.

rsus factory, 6,000 people were murdered here (Public Domain)

Shortly after their advance toward the center of Warsaw began, the two lead battle groups — Kampfgruppe "Rohr" (led by Generalmajor Günter Rohr) and Kampfgruppe "Reinefarth" (led by Heinz Reinefarth) — were halted by heavy fire from Polish resistance fighters. Unable to proceed forward, some of the German troops began to go from house to house carrying out their orders to shoot all inhabitants. Many civilians were shot on the spot, but some were killed after torture and sexual assault. Estimates vary, but Reinefarth himself has estimated that up to 10,000 civilians were killed in the Wola district on 5 August alone, the first day of the operation. Most of the victims were the elderly, women and children.

The majority of these atrocities were committed by troops under the command of SS-Oberführer Oskar Dirlewanger and SS-Brigadeführer Bronislav Kaminski.

Also on August 5, the Zośka battalion of the Home Army had managed to liberate the Gęsiówka concentration camp and to take control of the strategically important surrounding area of the former Warsaw Ghetto with the aid of two captured Panther tanks. Over the next few days of fighting this area became one of the main communication links between Wola and Warsaw's Old Town district, allowing insurrectionists and civilians to gradually withdraw from Wola ahead of the German forces that had been deployed against them.

On August 7, the German ground forces were strengthened further. To enhance their effectiveness, the Germans began to use civilians as human shields when approaching positions held by the Polish resistance. These tactics combined with their superior numbers and firepower helped them to fight their way to the Bank Square in the northern part of Warsaw's city center and cut the Wola district in half.

The Germans burned down two local hospitals with some of the patients still inside. Hundreds of other patients and personnel were killed by indiscriminate gunfire and grenade attacks or by executions. The greatest number of killings took place at the railway embankment on Górczewska Street and two large factories: the Ursus Factory and the Franaszka Factory - as well as the Pfeiffer Factory. In each of these four locations, thousands of people were systematically executed in mass shootings, having been previously rounded up in other places and taken there in groups.

Between August 8th and 23rd the SS formed groups of men from the Wola district into the so-called Verbrennungs Kommando ("burning detachment"), who were forced to hide evidence of the massacre by burning the victims' bodies and homes. Most of the men who were put to work in such groups were later executed.

The policy was designed to crush the Poles' will to fight and put the uprising to an end without having to commit to heavy city fighting. With time, the Germans realized that atrocities only stiffened resistance and that some political solution should be found, as the thousands of men at the disposal of the German commander were unable to effectively counter the resistance in an urban guerrilla setting.

On August 12, the order was given to stop the indiscriminate killing of civilians in Wola. Erich von dem Bach issued a new directive stating that captured civilians were to be evacuated from the city and deported to concentration camps or to labor camps.

BATTLE FOR OLD TOWN

Despite the loss of Wola, the Polish resistance strengthened. The insurgents managed to capture the ruins of the Warsaw Ghetto and liberate the Gęsiówka concentration camp, freeing about 350 Jews. On August 7, German forces were strengthened by the arrival of tanks using civilians as human shields. However, by then the net of barricades, street fortifications, and tank obstacles were already well-prepared; both sides reached a stalemate, with heavy house-to-house fighting.

arricade (Public Domain)

Between August 9 and 18 pitched battles raged around the Old Town with successful attacks by the Germans and counterattacks from the Poles. German tactics hinged on bombardment through the use of heavy artillery and tactical bombers, against which the Poles were unable to effectively defend themselves, as they lacked anti-aircraft weapons. Even clearly marked hospitals were bombed by dive-bombers, Stuka.

The Poles held the Old Town until a decision to withdraw was made at the end of August. On successive nights until September 2, the defenders of the Old Town withdrew through the sewers, which were a major means of communication between different parts of the city. Thousands of people were evacuated in this way. Those that remained were either shot or transported to concentration camps like Mauthausen and Sachsenhausen once the Germans regained control.

BATTLES IN OTHER DISTRICTS

Until August 11 - that is, until Wola and Ochota defended themselves - the Downtown did not feel the enemy's pressure directly. Although there were the main forces of the Warsaw AK District there, around 17,000 fighters, their commander, Col. "Monter", for a while was not inclined to take any offensive actions. In the first half of August, downtown troops concentrated on strengthening their positions and building a logistics base. It was not until the evening of August 13 that the AK units hit Mirow Market, intending to break through to the Old Town. The attack, however, ended in failure, prompting "Monter" to stop the attacks on the flank of von Dem Bach's main forces that were storming the Old Town. Instead, he developed the concept of the so-called maneuver from the south. Its main goal would be for the insurgents to break up the German forces defending the "police district". That would allow to obtain a ground connection between insurgent positions in the Downtown and Mokotów districts, after which the Warsaw units, strengthened by partisan units from the nearby forests, could stage a decisive battle for the liberation of the capital. The concept of "maneuver from the south" was very bold, but it required appropriate forces, resources, and above all time. All of those things the insurgents were lacking. To make matters worse, "Monter" busy with his plans was too late to realize that the battle for the Old Town is the main battle for the entire uprising and, as a result, neglected to provide adequate support for the defenders of the district.

At the end of August, the lack of weapons and ammunition, the deteriorating situation of the Old Town and the failed attacks on the German positions in the Southern Downtown disrupted the concept of "maneuver from the south." Before this happened, however, the Downtown squads carried out a series of limited offensive actions aimed at eliminating the German resistance points inside the district. After fierce battles, AK soldiers managed to overrun several German outposts, including the Police Headquarters with the nearby church of St. Cross. However, their threefold attacks against the Warsaw University complex, where German weapons and ammunition warehouses were located, were unsuccessful. In addition, after many days of clashes (between August 10 and 25), the insurgents managed to secure the corridor connecting Northern and Southern parts of Downtown. During this period of time, German offensive actions against the city center were of limited character and were undertaken primarily to secure access to the Wola freeway.

erman mobile assault gun (Public domain)

There were attempts to break the German ring around Warsaw by 2,000 forestry partisans on the night of August 18-19. However, they ended with moderate success. Only about 500 AK soldiers managed to break through to Mokotów. The losses were very large. Until August 22, Mokotów units managed to obtain a large (over 9 square kilometers) area of Sielec, Sadyba and the village of Czerniaków. Soon, it turned out, however, that the Polish forces were too weak to be able to defend the acquired territory and at the same time conduct offensive actions towards Downtown.

During this period no major clashes took place in Żoliborz. Even artillery and German air force, occupied in other parts of the city, rarely attacked the district. The only exception to this rule were unsuccessful attempts to gain the Gdansk Railway Station, in which the main role was played by units that arrived from the Kampinos Forest.

BERLING'S LANDING

The Soviet armies under the command of Konstantin Rokossovsky captured Praga and arrived on the east bank of the Vistula in mid-September. By September 13, the Germans had destroyed the remaining bridges over the Vistula and abandoned all their positions east of the river. In the Praga area fought Polish units of the First Polish Army under the command of General Berling, who were part of the Soviet 1st Belorussian Front. Three patrols of Berling's army landed on the shore of the Czerniaków and Powiśle areas and made contact with Home Army. The Red Army declined to support the Polish troops with artillery, tanks or bombers. They could not effectively counter enemy machine-gun fire as they crossed the river, and the landing troops sustained heavy losses. Only small elements of the main units made it ashore (I and III battalions of a 9th infantry regiment, 3rd Infantry Division).

Soldiers of First Polish Army prepare to cross Vistula River

The Germans intensified their attacks on the Home Army positions near the river to prevent any further landings, which could seriously compromise their line of defense, but weren't able to make any significant advances for several days, while Polish forces held those vital positions in preparation for new expected wave of Soviet landings. Polish units from the eastern shore attempted several more landings, and during the next few days sustained heavy losses (including destruction of all landing boats and most other river crossing equipment). Other Soviet units limited their assistance to sporadic and insignificant artillery and air support.

Shortly after the Berling's units' landings, the Soviets decided to postpone all plans for a river crossing in Warsaw "for at least 4 months" and soon afterwards general Berling was relieved of his command. On the night of September 19, after no further attempts from the other side of the river were made and the promised evacuation of the wounded did not take place, Home Army soldiers and landed elements of Polish Forces were forced to begin a retreat from their positions on the bank of the river.

Out of approximately 3,000 men who made it ashore only around 900 made it back to the eastern shores of the Vistula, approximately 600 of them seriously wounded.

Berling's Polish Army losses in an attempt to aid the Uprising were 5,660 killed, missing or wounded. From this point on, the Warsaw Uprising can be seen as a one-sided war of attrition or, alternatively, as a fight for acceptable terms of surrender. The Poles were besieged in three areas of the city: Śródmieście, Żoliborz and Mokotów.

BATTLES AROUND WARSAW

On August 14, 1944, the commander of the Home Army, general Tadeusz Komorowski, issued an order instructing all AK units around the occupied Poland to organize relief for Warsaw. The first units to attempt to bring relief to Warsaw were from the Kielce district, 110 miles away from Warsaw, in the strength of approximately 5,000 soldiers. From Lodz district (85 miles) marched the 25th Infantry Regiment, about 800 fighters. Groups from the Silesian district (150 miles), Rzeszów sub-district (195 miles), and the Lublin district (105 miles) did not manage to reach Warsaw. Partizan groups were attacked and stopped by German and Soviet troops. A 500-strong unit of Kedyw fighters (elite AK) set off from the Cracow district (180 miles) and made it to the vicinity of Częstochowa. On August 19, Kielce troops arrived in the Przysucha forests, 80 miles away from Warsaw, where it was decided that due to the lack of heavy weapons and difficulties in movement, reaching Warsaw was impossible. Nevertheless, these units throughout the September and October fought heavy battles with the Germans.

K unit in Kampinos Forest (Public Domain)

After the outbreak of the uprising, the battles also included the Kampinos Forest where the forest partisans joined forces with AK units from Warsaw. On the eve of the uprising, the structures of the Home Army could put up two infantry battalions, around 1,400 people, with only about 350-400 soldiers armed. After August 1, in the Kampinoska Forest, there were still small AK units from various districts of Warsaw, which left the city after the failures suffered in the "W" hour. A partisan group called the "Kampinos" Group was formed in mid-August. At its peak it had about 2,700 soldiers and 700 horses.

At the end of August, the Kampinos Group took control of the central and eastern areas of the Kampinos Forest, inhabited by several thousand people. The was named "The Independent Kampinos Republic". Its informal capital was Wiersze, where the headquarters of the grouping was located. Between July 29 and September 29, 1944, the "Kampinos" Group fought 47 battles with the Germans, with ten clashes ending in a clear victory for the Poles, and in thirteen cases the losses of the enemy far outweighed the losses of the insurgents. They also successfully clashed with units of the infamous SS Sturmbrigade RONA, a collaborationist formation composed of Russian nationals. By binding strong German forces for two months, the "Kampinos" Group relieved insurgent Warsaw. The presence of a strong partisan grouping in the forest also prevented the Germans from using safe and convenient forest routes leading to Warsaw and created a threat to the important German communication line which was the Warsaw - Modlin highway.

However, the activities of the "Kampinos" Group failed to change the fate of the uprising. After unsuccessful attacks on the Bielany airport (1-2 August), the Kampinos units were forced to retreat into the forest and until mid-August were unable to conduct offensive operations. After receiving an airdrop of weapons, ammunition and other supplies, the "Kampinos" Group, as the only organized AK group was able to send to the capital 900 well-armed soldiers.

The Germans finally blocked the routes between the "Kampinos Republic" and Warsaw. After that time, the Home Army recognized that they can no longer count on the arrival of relief or supplies.

On September 27, 1944 The Germans began a large-scale anti-partisan operation. In accordance with previous plans, the Kampinos Group then began to retreat towards the Świętokrzyskie Mountains. On October 1st the Kampinos Group suffered defeat in the battle with the German 9th army. Around 1,200 were killed and 460 wounded, 804 were taken prisoners. According to different reports a total of around 400 fighters survived either by joining other groups or by hiding in the forest awaiting a front line to pass.

AIRDROPS

From August 4 the Western Allies begun supporting the Uprising with airdrops of munitions and other supplies. Initially the flights were carried out mostly by the 1568th Polish Special Duties unit of the Polish Air Force stationed in Bari and Brindisi in Italy, flying B-24 Liberator, Handley Page Halifax and Douglas C-47 Dakota planes. Later on, at the insistence of the Polish government-in-exile, they were joined by the Liberators of No.31 and No. 34 Squadrons of the South African Air Force based in Foggia in Southern Italy, and Halifaxes, flown by No. 148 and No. 178 RAF Squadrons. The drops by British, Polish and South African forces continued until September 21. The total weight of allied drops was about 230 tons, over 200 flights were made.

The Soviet Union did not allow the Western Allies to use its airports for the airdrops for several weeks, so the planes had to use bases in the United Kingdom and Italy which reduced their carrying weight and number of sorties. The Allies' specific request for the use of landing strips made on August 20 was denied by Stalin on August 22. Stalin referred to the Polish resistance as "a handful of criminals" and stated that the Uprising was inspired by "enemies of the Soviet Union". Thus, by denying landing rights to Allied aircraft on Soviet-controlled territory the Soviets vastly limited effectiveness of Allied assistance to the Uprising, and even fired at Allied airplanes which carried supplies from Italy and strayed into Soviet-controlled airspace.

rew of B-24 Liberator that flew over Warsaw

American support was also limited. After Stalin's objections to supporting the uprising, British Prime Minister Winston Churchill telegraphed U.S. President Franklin D. Roosevelt on August 25 and proposed sending planes in defiance of Stalin, to "see what happens". Unwilling to upset Stalin before the Yalta Conference, Roosevelt replied on August 26: "I do not consider it advantageous to the long-range general war prospect for me to join you".

Finally, on September 18 the Soviets allowed a USAAF flight of 107 B-17 Flying Fortresses of the Eighth Air Force's 3rd Division to re-fuel and reload at Soviet airfields used in Operation Frantic, but it was too little too late. The planes dropped 100 tons of supplies, but only 20 were recovered by the resistance due to the wide area over which they were spread. The vast majority of supplies fell into German-held areas. The USAAF lost two B-17s with a further seven damaged. The aircraft landed at the Operation Frantic air bases in the Soviet Union, where they were rearmed and refueled, and the next day 100 B-17s and 61 P-51s left the USSR to bomb the marshalling yard at Szolnok in Hungary on their way back to bases in Italy. Soviet intelligence reports show that Soviet commanders on the ground near Warsaw estimated that 96% of the supplies dropped by the Americans fell into German hands. From the Soviet perspective, the Americans were supplying the Nazis instead of aiding the Polish resistance. The Soviets refused permission for any further American flights until September 30, by which time the weather was too poor to fly, and the Uprising was nearly over.

Between September 13 and September 30 Soviet aircraft commenced their own re-supply missions, dropping arms, medicines and food supplies. Initially, these supplies were dropped in canisters without parachutes which led to damage and loss of the contents. Also, a large number of canisters fell into German hands.

Although German air defense over the Warsaw area was almost non-existent, about 12% of the 296 planes taking part in the operations were lost because they had to fly 990 miles out and the same distance back over heavily defended enemy territory (112 out of 637 Polish and 133 out of 735 British and South African airmen were shot down). Most of the drops were made during the night, at no more than 100–300 ft altitude, and poor accuracy left many parachuted packages stranded behind German-controlled territory (only about 50 tons of supplies, less than 50% delivered, was recovered by the resistance).

It is needless to say that the airdrops as an operation was a disaster that could be blamed on the lack of moral spine on the part of Prime Minister Churchill and President Roosevelt (in particular) in their dealings with Russian dictator, Stalin.

CAPITULATION

By the first week of September both German and Polish commanders realized that the Soviet army was unlikely to act. The Germans reasoned that a prolonged Uprising would damage their ability to hold Warsaw as the front line; the Poles were concerned that continued resistance would result in further massive casualties. On September 7, General Rohr proposed negotiations, which Bór-Komorowski agreed to pursue the following day.

gning of documents ending all fighting (Public Domain)

Over two days, September 8-10, about 20,000 civilians were evacuated by agreement of both sides, and Rohr recognized the right of Home Army soldiers to be treated as military combatants. The Poles suspended talks on the 11th, as they received the news that the Soviets were advancing slowly through Praga. A few days later, the arrival of the 1st Polish army breathed new life into the resistance and the talks collapsed.

However, by the morning of September 27, the Germans had retaken Warsaw's district, Mokotów. Talks resumed on September 28. On the evening of September 30, Żoliborz fell to the Germans. The Poles were being pushed back into fewer and fewer streets, and their situation was ever more desperate. On the 30th, Hitler decorated von dem Bach, Dirlewanger and Reinefarth, while in London, General Sosnkowski was dismissed as Polish commander-in-chief. Bór-Komorowski was promoted in his place, even though he was trapped in Warsaw. Bór-Komorowski and Prime Minister Mikołajczyk again appealed directly to Rokossovsky and Stalin for a Soviet intervention. None came. According to Soviet Marshal Georgy Zhukov, who was by this time at the Vistula front, both he and

Rokossovsky advised Stalin against an offensive because of heavy Soviet losses.

The capitulation order of the remaining Polish forces was finally signed on October 2nd. All fighting ceased that evening. According to the agreement, the Wehrmacht promised to treat Home Army soldiers in accordance with the Geneva Convention, and to treat the civilian population humanely.

The next day the Germans began to disarm the Home Army soldiers. They later sent 15,000 of them to POW camps in various parts of Germany. Between 5,000 and 6,000 resistance fighters decided to blend into the civilian population hoping to continue the fight later. The entire civilian population of Warsaw was expelled from the city and sent to a transit camp Durchgangslager 121 in Pruszków. Out of 350,000–550,000 civilians who passed through the camp, 90,000 were sent to labor camps in the Third Reich, 60,000 were shipped to death and concentration camps (including Ravensbrück, Auschwitz, Mauthausen, among others), while the rest were transported to various locations in the General Government.

The Soviets made no attempt to push forward, until the Vistula–Oder Offensive began on January 12, 1945. In the time between the capitulation and "liberation", nearly three months, the city was systematically and almost entirely destroyed Warsaw by Germans. It was "liberated" on January 17, 1945 by the Red Army and the First Polish Army.

Most soldiers of the Home Army (including those who took part in the Warsaw Uprising) were persecuted after the war; captured by the NKVD (now KGB) or UB (Polish secret police). They were interrogated and imprisoned on various charges, such as that of fascism. Many of them were sent to the Gulags, executed or disappeared.

AFTERMATH

Polish losses
- 10,000 insurgents killed.
- 6,000 missing (MIA).
- 25,000 insurgents injured, including 6,500 seriously injured.
- 15,000 prisoners of war.
- 150,000 - 180,000 civilians killed. At least 30 percent of people who died during the Warsaw Uprising are victims of executions carried out by German police and military formations.

- 12 tons of ashes coming from the burned corpses of murdered Poles were collected in Wola district. Between 50,000 and 65,000 residents of that district were killed by the Nazis in the first two weeks of August.
- 600,000 - 650,000 deported from Warsaw, including 150,000 sent to labor and concentration camps.

German losses
- 10,000 troops killed.
- 7,000 KIAs.
- 7,500 - 9,000 injured.
- 2,000 prisoners of war.
- Unknown number of civilians.

DESTRUCTION OF THE CITY

icture of Warsaw in 1950 (Public Domain)

The destruction of Warsaw was actually a methodical razing of the city. The uprising had infuriated German leaders, who decided to make an example of the city, which they had long since selected for major demolition as part of their planned Germanization of Central Europe.

"The city must completely disappear from the surface of the earth and serve only as a transport station for the Wehrmacht. No stone can remain standing. Every building must be razed to its foundation" - SS chief Heinrich Himmler.

"Warsaw has to be pacified, that is, razed to the ground" - Adolf Hitler.

Even before the uprising, the Germans knew that, within a few months, Warsaw would fall into Allied hands. Despite that, they dedicated an unprecedented effort to destroying the city. Their decision tied up considerable resources which could have been used on the Eastern Front and in the newly opened Western Front following the Normandy landings.

After the remaining population had been expelled, the Germans continued the destruction of the city. Special groups of German engineers were dispatched to burn and demolish the remaining buildings. The demolition squads used flamethrowers and explosives to methodically destroy house after house. They paid special attention to historical monuments, Polish national archives, museums and places of interest.

d Town district of Warsaw in January 1945 (Public Domain)

Material losses are estimated at 10,455 buildings, 923 historical buildings (94%), 25 churches, 14 libraries, including the National Library, 81 primary schools, 64 high schools, University of Warsaw and Warsaw University of Technology, and most of the historical monuments. Almost a million inhabitants lost all of their possessions. The exact amount of losses of private and public property as well as pieces of art, monuments of science and culture is unknown but considered enormous.

By January 1945, 85%-90% of the buildings were destroyed.

On the 1st of January 1945 Warsaw had no more than 1,000 inhabitants.

ABOUT THE AUTHOR

Kris lives with his family in Connecticut. His other passions are: medieval history of Poland and Yoga. He is also an author of "Yoga for Men in 5 Minutes." He is also a publisher of PoloniaNews.com.

REFERENCES AND EXTERNAL LINKS

The official website of this book - KillingWarsaw.com

The Warsaw Rising Museum - www.1944.pl/en

Warsaw Uprising - en.wikipedia.org/wiki/Warsaw_Uprising

Warsaw Uprising 1944 - www.warsawuprising.com

Home Army - en.wikipedia.org/wiki/Home_Army

Warsaw Ghetto Uprising - en.wikipedia.org/wiki/Warsaw_Ghetto_Uprising

Warsaw Ghetto - en.wikipedia.org/wiki/Warsaw_Ghetto

Underground State - en.wikipedia.org/wiki/Polish_Underground_State

How Warsaw Came Close to Never Being Rebuilt
https://culture.pl/en/article/how-warsaw-came-close-to-never-being-rebuilt

The Destruction and Rebuilding of Warsaw
https://historynewsnetwork.org/blog/153807

The Destruction of Warsaw: The Nazi Plan to Obliterate A City
https://www.history.co.uk/article/the-destruction-of-warsaw-the-nazi-plan-to-obliterate-a-city

More resources, including videos can be found at www.killingwarsaw.com

Made in the USA
Middletown, DE
21 October 2021

49991914R00050